Winning at Human Relations

How to Keep from Sabotaging Yourself

DISCARD

Revised Edition

Elwood N. Chapman
and Barb Wingfield

D1378727

A Fifty-Minute™ Series Book

This Fifty-Minute™ book is designed to be "read with a pencil." It is an excellent workbook for self-study as well as classroom learning. All material is copyright-protected and cannot be duplicated without permission from the publisher. *Therefore, be sure to order a copy for every training participant by contacting:*

1-800-442-7477

Menlo Park, CA
www.crisplearning.com

Winning at Human Relations

How to Keep from Sabotaging Yourself

Revised Edition

**Elwood N. Chapman
and Barb Wingfield**

CREDITS:
Senior Editor: **Debbie Woodbury**
Editor: **Ann Gosch**
Assistant Editor: **Genevieve Del Rosario**
Production Manager: **Judy Petry**
Design: **Nicole Phillips**
Production Design: **Rich Lehl**
Cartoonist: **Ralph Mapson**

© 1989, 2003 Crisp Publications, Inc.
Printed in the United States of America by Von Hoffmann Graphics, Inc.

www.crisplearning.com

03 04 05 10 9 8 7 6 5 4 3 2

Library of Congress Catalog Card Number 2002115414
Chapman, Elwood N. and Barb Wingfield
Winning at Human Relations
ISBN 1-56052-689-0

Learning Objectives For:

WINNING AT HUMAN RELATIONS

The objectives for *Winning at Human Relations, Revised Edition* are listed below. They have been developed to guide you, the reader, to the core issues covered in this book.

THE OBJECTIVES OF THIS BOOK ARE:

❑ 1) To explain human relations principles as they apply to career success

❑ 2) To present tips for successful communication

❑ 3) To teach strategies for improving relationships with co-workers and supervisors

❑ 4) To advise on how to keep from sabotaging yourself

❑ 5) To explore ways to repair damaged relationships

ASSESSING YOUR PROGRESS

In addition to the learning objectives, Crisp Learning has developed an **assessment** that covers the fundamental information presented in this book. A 25-item, multiple-choice and true-false questionnaire allows the reader to evaluate his or her comprehension of the subject matter. To buy the assessment and answer key, go to www.crisplearning.com and search on the book title, or call 1-800-442-7477.

Assessments should not be used in any employee selection process.

About the Authors

The late Elwood N. Chapman retired in 1977 as a professor at Chaffey College and a visiting lecturer at Claremont Graduate School after 29 years of successful teaching. He was a graduate of the University of California. Mr. Chapman was also the co-founder of Crisp Publications and author of more than a dozen books by Crisp.

Barb Wingfield, founder of Morale Builders, works with businesses to provide a work environment where employees can flourish. A member of the National Speakers Association and the National Association for Employee Recognition, she presents keynotes, conducts training, and provides consulting throughout the United States. Ms. Wingfield is the author of *Reasons to Say WOW!!! A Celebration of Life's Simple Pleasures* and co-author of the Crisp book, *Retaining Your Employees: Using Respect Recognition and Rewards for Positive Results.* She can be reached by e-mail at barb@moralebuilders.com or via her Web site at www.moralebuilders.com

How to Use This Book

This *Fifty-Minute™ Series Book* is a unique, user-friendly product. As you read through the material, you will quickly experience the interactive nature of the book. There are numerous exercises, real-world case studies, and examples that invite your opinion, as well as checklists, tips, and concise summaries that reinforce your understanding of the concepts presented.

A Crisp Learning *Fifty-Minute™ Book* can be used in a variety of ways. Individual self-study is one of the most common. However, many organizations use *Fifty-Minute* books for pre-study before a classroom training session. Other organizations use the books as a part of a systemwide learning program—supported by video and other media based on the content in the books. Still others work with Crisp Learning to customize the material to meet their specific needs and reflect their culture. Regardless of how it is used, we hope you will join the more than 20 million satisfied learners worldwide who have completed a *Fifty-Minute Book.*

Preface

The relationships you create and maintain with others, whether in your career or personal life, should be viewed as treasures. They are the jewels of living. When relationships are healthy, open, fun, and mutually rewarding, they can enrich your life far beyond material possessions. Good relationships will sustain you in hard times.

But interpersonal human dealings are fragile and demand tender loving care. Even when they seem strong, they can never be taken for granted. Those who become skillful at creating and maintaining ongoing positive relationships enjoy more successful careers and happier personal lives. We sometimes refer to these individuals as being human-relations smart.

Although this book's emphasis is career or working relationships, all ideas, principles, and techniques can be applied to your personal life. Good luck as you learn to "win at human relations."–*Elwood N. Chapman*

Every day we are involved in many aspects of human relations. Some of us excel while others struggle to interact with people in a positive way. The late Elwood Chapman's years of experience in working with people on several levels provided a rich foundation for this book and the many others he wrote.

It was a great honor to revise this book. The core concepts are still fundamentally sound. The greatest change in the book was choosing different words to communicate the importance of recognizing behaviors that can lead to self-sabotage. The examples were changed to create more current work situations, to enable you, the reader, to apply it to your life. I have focused on the importance of building relationships and highlighted trigger points that can weaken relationships.

As you read this book, choose the ideas and tips that are best suited to your situation and form a plan of how you will best use the information. Plan for success and you will be a winner at human relations. Enjoy the journey.

–*Barb Wingfield*

Acknowledgments

I would like to thank Paula Butterfield, Ph.D., for her help and encouragement on this project. Her wisdom and caring about the revisions were very valuable. I would also like to thank Michael Brickey, Ph.D., for his insight into the content changes. A special thanks to my cheerleaders in life: Bob, Shirley, Julie, and Robin.

Contents

Part 3: Protecting Yourself from Self-Sabotage

Part 4: Putting It All Together into a Winning Strategy

Appendix

Introduction

Organizations pay a monumental price in lost productivity because of emotional disturbances and negative attitudes caused by damaged interpersonal relationships. A conflict between employees, especially at the executive level, can not only affect the decision-making process, but also sometimes destroy the morale of an entire organization.

In areas where solid customer relations are essential, human-relations conflicts can damage or destroy key client relationships. Human conflicts are also a primary cause of employee turnover. With recruitment, employment, and training costs as high as they are, this factor alone can drain the resources of any firm.

Employees lower their personal productivity, and that of their co-workers, when they bring outside personal conflicts to work.

Obviously, those who understand and practice positive human-relations skills contribute not only to their organizations but also to their personal career progress. The objective of this book is to help readers build and maintain positive human relationships.

Understanding Human Relations Skills

It is human nature to think wisely and act foolishly."

—**Anatole France**

2

Recognizing the Importance of Human Relations

More careers have been damaged through faulty human relations skills than through a lack of technical ability. Many people are technically smart, but human-relations dumb, because they seem unaware that simply knowing how to do a job is not the key to success. To produce results, most of us depend on others and this requires knowing how to work with people. Before this can be done successfully, many human relations skills must be learned and practiced.

Many individuals underestimate the problems that poor human relations can cause. They persist in concentrating on personal productivity and ignore the fact that they are part of a complicated *team* structure that can operate efficiently only when human relationships are given proper attention.

To be human-relations smart, it is essential to maintain cooperative relationships with all members of an organization, from co-workers to supervisors. Communication must be open and healthy. The quality of any relationship will influence the productivity from that individual.

When Khanh got her first office job, she concentrated almost all her attention on the accuracy and quantity of her work. Soon her productivity level was higher than any of her six co-workers and she made no secret of it to others. Did Khanh receive a compliment from her supervisor? Yes, but along with it, she was firmly reminded that she was part of a team, and "broadcasting" her output was causing resentment and hurting others' productivity.

Despite the excellent skills Khanh demonstrated, she had not learned to balance her technical competencies with good human relations, or that her dedicated efforts to achieve personal goals could have a negative impact on the productivity of others. She was blind to the bigger picture that involves building and maintaining good relationships with both co-workers and supervisors.

TEST YOUR HUMAN RELATIONS "SMARTS"

Although human-relations skills are not as easy to identify or quantify as technical skills, they are extremely important to career progress. The more you practice positive human relations, the less often co-workers and supervisors will misinterpret your goals and the more supportive they will be.

Listed below are 20 human-relations competencies. Check (✔) only those you practice daily. This exercise will demonstrate why it is difficult to be *human-relations smart.*

I consistently:

❑ Deal with all people in an honest, ethical, and moral way.

❑ Remain positive and upbeat even while working with others who may be negative.

❑ Send out positive verbal and nonverbal signals in all human interactions, including the telephone.

❑ Refuse to be involved in any activity that might be hurtful or damaging to another person.

❑ Build and maintain open and healthy working relationships with everyone in the workplace. I refuse to play favorites.

❑ Treat everyone, regardless of ethnic or socioeconomic differences, with respect.

❑ Work effectively with others regardless of their sexual orientation.

❑ Am open to others to restore a damaged relationship with me. I focus on a positive outcome.

❑ Maintain a strong relationship with my immediate supervisor without alienating co-workers.

CONTINUED

☑ Am a better-than-average producer while contributing to the productivity of co-workers.

☑ Refuse to initiate or circulate potentially harmful rumors.

☐ Maintain a good attendance record, including being on time to work.

☑ Show I can live up to my productivity potential without alienating co-workers who do not live up to theirs.

☑ Acknowledge mistakes or misjudgments rather than hide them.

☑ Refuse to allow small gripes to grow into major upsets.

☑ Am an excellent listener.

☑ Keep a good balance between my home and career lives so that neither suffers.

☑ Look for and appreciate the good characteristics of others.

☑ Keep my business and personal relationships sufficiently separated.

☑ Make only positive comments about those not present.

Scoring:

Give yourself five points for each square checked.

A score of 70 or more indicates you are practicing a substantial number of recognized human-relations skills; a score of 50 or less suggests a review of current practices is in order.

Focusing on the Relationship, Not the Personality

The most objective way to view human interaction is to concentrate on the relationship itself–consider it to be a conduit or connection between people–and try to forget the personalities on either end. When you focus on the relationship rather than worry about personalities, you can be more objective.

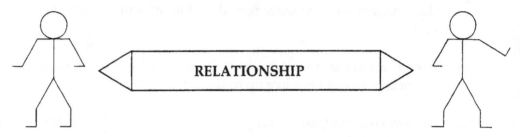

Some people find this impossible to do. As a result, they are unable to get beyond personality traits they consider irritating. Result: A personality conflict often develops and the productivity of both parties and those surrounding them is damaged unnecessarily.

Although relationships usually reflect personalities at each end of the line, concentrating on the relationship itself helps people ignore irritating mannerisms and concentrate instead on the potential productivity of the interaction. Concentrating on the relationship rather than personalities also helps some people minimize differences in age or values, ethnic background, or sexual orientation. Too often these factors negatively affect an individual's ability to see the bigger picture. When people are able to push such matters aside and deal exclusively with the relationship itself, greater objectivity and fairness will result and things will move in a more positive direction.

It is a difficult lesson to learn, but individuals who allow the personality of another to irritate them into a negative attitude are the ones who suffer. Away from work, basing a personal relationship on personality is expected. The workplace, however–where productivity hinges on positive relationships–is a different matter.

CASE STUDY: DOWNPLAYING A PERSONALITY CONFLICT

Jeff had invested almost 20 years with a growing, progressive firm. He was proud of his vice presidency, excellent salary, and strong benefits. Recently, though, Jeff had permitted himself to fall into an intense personality conflict with the new president. Jeff no longer looked forward to his work, and his wife Nancy grew increasingly concerned about her husband's emotional health. As a result, she persuaded Jeff to seek professional counseling.

The counselor suggested that Jeff could make progress solving his problem by shifting the focus away from the president's demanding personality toward the working relationship between them. Jeff got the message. Later, he and Nancy decided it would help to list the president's most irritating characteristics on a piece of paper and then burn it in the fireplace. They reasoned that by doing so, Jeff could concentrate on his productivity and not worry about being frustrated by the president's behavior. Jeff said to himself: "Why allow the strange personality of my boss to affect my work and career?"

What chance do you give the strategy of working?

      Excellent chance   ❏

      No chance   ❏

      Worth trying   ❏

How would you handle the situation?

_____

_____

_____

_____

*Compare your answers to the authors' suggested
responses in the back of the book.*

Possessing a Positive Attitude

In the work environment, as in your personal life, nothing contributes more to building and maintaining healthy relationships than a positive attitude.

What Is a Positive Attitude?

Attitude is your general disposition—your mental starting point for viewing life and the people and events in it. From your viewpoint, attitude is the way you look at things mentally, and it all starts inside your head. For others, your attitude is the overall mood they interpret from what they see you say and do.

On your way to work, think of attitude as the mental focus that you have toward the day ahead. Like using a camera, you can focus your mind either on the positive or negative factors that exist. You can view your work station as an interesting place where you can grow, learn, accomplish career goals, and have some fun; or it can be a drag from the time you arrive until you leave. Perception—the complicated process of viewing and interpreting your environment—is a mental phenomenon. It is within your power to concentrate on selected aspects of your work environment and ignore others. Quite simply, you take the picture you want to take of your job and career.

Why Does Attitude Make Such a Big Difference?

A positive attitude will accomplish three basic goals:

> ➤ It will trigger your enthusiasm toward your work and the people surrounding you.

> ➤ It will enhance your creativity and put you in a position to increase your productivity.

> ➤ It will help you make the most of your personality.

When you have a positive attitude, co-workers find it easier to build a relationship with you and are motivated to keep it healthy and alive longer.

But as important as attitude may be, it is the combination of attitude and solid human-relations skills that spells career success.

> *A happy person is not a person in a certain set of circumstances, but rather, one with a certain set of attitudes."*
>
> **–Hugh Downs**

This content was used with permission from *Attitude: Your Most Priceless Possession,* by Elwood N. Chapman and Wil McKnight, by Crisp Publications.

GAUGE YOUR ATTITUDE

This exercise is designed to help you measure whether you are making a strong effort to achieve the best possible work attitude. If you circle a *10*, you are saying you make the supreme effort each day; if you circle a *1*, you are saying you have given up on making any attitude improvement in this area. Be honest.

	HIGH (Positive)	LOW (Negative)

1. I concentrate on adjusting my attitude each morning on my way to work.　　10 9 8 7 6 5 4 3 2 1

2. If I were to guess, I believe my supervisor would rate my attitude as a...　　10 9 8 7 6 5 4 3 2 1

3. I make a serious effort each day to build positive working relationships with all my co-workers.　　10 9 8 7 6 5 4 3 2 1

4. I believe my co-workers would rate my current attitude as a...　　10 9 8 7 6 5 4 3 2 1

5. If a meter could gauge my sense of humor in the workplace, it would read close to a...　　10 9 8 7 6 5 4 3 2 1

6. I rate my enthusiasm toward my current job as a...　　10 9 8 7 6 5 4 3 2 1

7. I never permit little things to negatively influence my positive attitude.　　10 9 8 7 6 5 4 3 2 1

8. I would rate the attitude I communicate over the telephone as a...　　10 9 8 7 6 5 4 3 2 1

9. The patience and sensitivity I show to others, inside or outside of any organization, deserves a rating of...　　10 9 8 7 6 5 4 3 2 1

10. Based on my work performance and general attitude, I deserve a...　　10 9 8 7 6 5 4 3 2 1

TOTAL _____

Scoring:

A score of 90 or more is a signal that you are doing an outstanding job in human relations. A score between 70 and 90 indicates your attitude is good and you demonstrate you are human-relations smart. A rating between 50 and 70 suggests an improvement in your attitude would measurably improve your working relationships. If you rated yourself below 50, your human-relations progress is severely restricted by your attitude.

Leveling the Workload

In any team situation, every person is expected to carry a fair share of the workload. Managers have the responsibility of evaluating the individual contribution of team members. It is natural for some individuals to carry a slightly heavier load because of ability, experience, motivation, or pride. Small productivity imbalances are no problem. But when a gap becomes noticeably excessive, team relationships often deteriorate.

Sometimes high producers become emotionally disturbed over the low productivity of others. As a result, high producers may sound off and lose the support of other team members or allow their own productivity to suffer. Result? Departmental productivity drops.

When John started his teaching career, his standards were so high that he permitted himself to become upset with colleagues who had measurably lower standards. After one year in the classroom he left for another career. Today he looks back and realizes that he would have been happier to remain in teaching. He freely acknowledges he permitted the behavior of others to chase him away from the career he really wanted.

For most employees, the solution to working with those who perform at lower levels is a three-step process:

1. Continue to set a good example and do your best to ignore the personal productivity of others. This is difficult because it may drag on indefinitely.

2. Resolve the problem through conflict-resolution techniques such as mutual understanding, bargaining, or collaboration of some kind.

3. Take the situation to a supervisor to resolve the imbalance. Ultimately a solution is necessary or the high producers—the employees management needs to keep—might leave. These high producers might rightfully perceive that under certain conditions, leaving is the best available choice.

Building Relationships with Co-Workers

Your most important working relationship is with your immediate supervisor. And most often, the best way to maintain an excellent relationship with your supervisor is to concentrate on improving relationships with your co-workers.

Why is this so?

Perceptive supervisors observe your ability to work well with co-workers because positive working relationships affect productivity. When supervisors notice you are able to build good relationships with team members, you automatically build good relationships with your supervisors.

When Jill started her new career with Mytech, she was friendly, open, and not the least bit intimidated by supervisors. Jill devoted most of her relationship-building time to her co-workers. Result? Her supervisors were impressed with her human-relations skills and the contribution she made to other team members. It paid off a year later when Jill was promoted to a supervisory role at another location.

Jill concentrated on co-worker relationships but did not neglect her other relationships. She did everything possible to maintain excellent relations with her immediate supervisor. She kept him informed and always made sure she provided follow-through on her projects. She was smart enough to know that any moves she made that might lead to favoritism from above could backfire. She simply let her skills at building positive relationships with others speak for her.

Maintaining Relationships Through Communication

Verbal communication between two people is usually the way an important relationship gets started.

The 20-year relationship between Brooke and Laura started when they found themselves in the same management-training program. Sharing experiences at the end of each day, they built a common bond that has lasted.

Regular communication—whether face-to-face or by e-mail, telephone, or letter—is almost always necessary to maintain a relationship over an extended period of time.

Within a year Brooke took her talents to another firm. She and Laura continued to maintain their relationship through frequent telephone calls, e-mails, and dinner meetings at least once a month. The bond between them strengthened as they provided mutual support and career-enhancement strategies to each other.

Immediate, open, face-to-face communication is the best way to restore a damaged relationship.

At one point, the two women had a falling out when Brooke rejoined Laura's company and was supervised by Laura. Brooke was not prepared for the more authoritative leadership style that Laura had developed since the "old days." It became necessary for Laura to initiate a one-on-one meeting where they discussed the problem openly. Thanks to sensitivity and mutual respect on both sides, their personal relationship became close again despite the new manager/employee association.

Laura and Brooke were human-relations smart because they learned to communicate, communicate, communicate! Like a delicate plant that is nurtured to maturity through water, fertilizer, and tender loving care, human relationships are nurtured through communication. The next time you hear of a relationship that has fallen apart, it would be safe to assume that a lack of communication played a significant role in the separation.

Practicing the Mutual Reward Theory

It is usually easy to initiate positive relationships in the workplace. The challenge comes in building and maintaining these relationships for the benefit of all concerned. One way to help this happen is to see that each individual receives rewards from the other party that are approximately equal in value. This simple *reward exchange* policy is the basis for the Mutual Reward Theory.

MRT reasons that for a relationship to remain healthy, both parties must benefit. That is, a voluntary, essentially equal exchange of benefits must exist between the two parties. The rewards need not be the same in kind or number, but when one person starts to receive more than he or she gives, the relationship is vulnerable.

Justin, new on the job, and Haines, with 10 years' seniority, started out with a promising working relationship. Justin, a recent graduate with excellent computer skills, was always willing to leave his work station and help Haines with his specialized computer applications. Haines, in turn, willingly provided Justin with insights on how to better understand the corporate culture. The relationship was mutually rewarding. But Justin was savvy at adapting to the company's culture and soon found that he did not need Haines's insight. Justin was now providing more of the giving and the relationship began to deteriorate. The mutually rewarding portion had disappeared.

For any relationship to remain healthy, both parties must appreciate the mutual exchange of benefits. It is therefore human-relations smart to make sure that the other party in any important relationship continues to receive appropriate rewards. In the above situation, if Justin withdrew his computer support, a possible solution might be for Haines to sit down with Justin and work out another "reward mix."

Controlling Reactions to Emotional Trigger Points

The way others treat you can cause you to react emotionally and damage an important relationship. Sometimes others may not realize their behavior is upsetting you. As a result, you may harm yourself if you are overly sensitive.

To help you avoid overreacting, rank the items listed below from 1 to 6, with *1* being the incident that would upset you most and *6* being the one that would upset you least.

I become upset when another person:

- ❏ Seems to ignore me at a gathering where others are present

- ❏ Fails to keep what I believe was a promise

- ❏ Holds back on information I feel I deserve to know

- ❏ Cancels an appointment

- ❏ Refuses to be a good listener

- ❏ Pays more attention to another person

If a working relationship is important, do not permit it to be damaged by situations similar to those listed above. Otherwise, your career may suffer while the offending party walks away, unaware of the damage that has occurred. Most of us have permitted an important relationship to deteriorate over a minor matter that was unintended by the other party. The best way to handle such situations is either to give the other person the benefit of the doubt or discuss the matter openly and clear the air.

Which will be your strategy?

- ❏ I intend to say nothing if a situation similar to those listed occurs. I will, however, be more tolerant and give the other party the benefit of the doubt. This means I will quickly forgive and forget.

- ❏ I plan to discuss potential misinterpretations immediately to clear the air and restore the relationship as quickly as possible. Talking it over will help improve communications.

Avoiding Absenteeism and Tardiness

One of the most frequent ways employees damage their relationships is through needless tardiness and absenteeism. Here is why:

➤ A poor attendance record builds a credibility gap with supervisors

➤ Frequent absence from responsibilities requires co-workers to pick up the slack

➤ Records that reflect heavy absenteeism and tardiness are permanent and can be evaluated by other managers reviewing internal candidates for promotion

➤ For layoffs, cutbacks, or reassignments, those with poor records are often the first to go

Despite such penalties, many capable employees fail to see how they damage relationships in all directions.

Rebecca was, without question, the most capable technician on the team. When she was on the job and on top of things, her productivity was exceptional. But Rebecca was frequently late and periodically absent. This caused problems for other team members because they had to adjust their work loads to offset Rebecca's lack of dependability.

Eventually, Rebecca's career was permanently damaged because of ongoing absenteeism. When asked about it, she replied: "I took a chance and lost. I didn't have to be late or absent; I just thought that I was good enough to get by with it. When my co-workers got tired of holding me up, the game was over.

Many otherwise clever people fail to see the human-relations aspects of being tardy or absent. By refusing to discipline themselves, their credibility is in question even when they have legitimate reasons for being late or away from work.

ARE YOUR ACTIONS BUILDING OR WEAKENING RELATIONSHIPS?

One way to create conflict within a relationship is to fail to provide the expected behavior to the other party. The column on the left lists behaviors that focus on building relationships. The column on the right demonstrates that when the same behaviors are absent, they become weakening points. Feel free to add your own.

Building Relationships	Weakening Relationships
Free and open communication	Minimal or poor communication
Accepting value differences	Prejudice
Carrying a full load	Failure to pull your expected weight
Balanced rewards	Unequal rewards
Trust	Lack of trust
Recognizing the independence of another	Jealousy
Sense of humor	Lack of humor
Sensitive to needs	Insensitive to needs
Generous (with time, talent, money, etc.)	Stingy beyond reason
Keeps others informed	Failure to inform
High on patience	Impatient
Keeps promises	Forgets promises
Seldom absent	Frequently absent
Excellent follow-through	Little follow-through
Handles own personal problems	Unloads on co-workers
Remains upbeat	Consistently negative
_____	_____
_____	_____

CASE STUDY: CONFLICTING RELATIONSHIPS

Jennifer, an experienced office professional, was immediately impressed with Victoria when she joined the department. Jennifer went out of her way to help Victoria feel comfortable in her new environment. As a result, Victoria introduced Jennifer to social friends away from work. Soon they were enjoying evenings out together and wound up sharing an apartment. It appeared, on the surface, to be a mutually rewarding arrangement. But after a few months, it became apparent that Victoria did not have a genuine interest in her job. Her productivity never improved and required substantial co-worker support.

Soon, to the surprise of others, Jennifer started making excuses for her friend. Although Jennifer had an excellent image and was considered management material before Victoria arrived, she was now viewed as a person with questionable judgment. Without being fully aware of what was happening, Jennifer began to sabotage herself in what had started to be a legitimate, mutually rewarding relationship. Looking back later, Jennifer made these comments:

"I made a serious human-relations mistake. My need to be more socially accepted and have a good time blinded me. In time, it became obvious that Victoria was hanging on to my work coattails and I was hanging on to her social coattails. Our reward system got out of line when she traded on my personal productivity and status to keep her job. When things got so bad that Victoria was terminated, I had to rebuild my image with co-workers and management. It won't happen again."

How could Jennifer have better built separate work and social relationships with Victoria?

_____

_____

How can Jennifer expand her self-awareness so she could avoid future challenges in building relationships?

_____

_____

Compare your answers to the authors' suggested responses in the back of the book.

Staying Focused During Career Plateaus

Each career path contains periods when an individual must "stand still" rather than move upward. Promotions may be in the future, but for now the organization can do nothing. This is known as a *plateau* period.

Such a period must be understood, because it can lead to negativity. And this can cause affected individuals to neglect their human-relations opportunities.

Because of slower-than-expected growth and some restructuring, management was aware that it would be a tough waiting period for Seth and Chavez. Both were counseled to be patient and continue to prepare for promotions that would eventually materialize. Chavez took these suggestions seriously and used the waiting period to improve relationships and upgrade his competencies. Seth, on the other hand, became discouraged and let things slip. When the environment improved, Chavez was promoted, but Seth was not ready. In talking it over with the director of human resources, Seth was told: "When you failed to stay positive, maintain relationships, and keep your personal productivity high, you disqualified yourself."

Plateau periods are never easy. It is difficult to keep learning and staying positive when you feel you are ready for more responsibility but nothing happens. Some occasions might call for activating a Plan B (see page 72). But for those who remain with the organization and want to progress, staying interested and involved is necessary to avoid career damage.

Balancing Career and Personal Problems

Winning in human relations requires maintaining the integrity of the work environment, no matter what might be going on at home. But work environments often serve as support systems when personal problems arise, so it is natural for co-workers to share such matters with one another on the job. The challenges are deciding how much to involve and share with co-workers and working to maintain your job performance so your career will not suffer. Each situation is unique, and each work environment and individual will handle the balance differently.

If you are having a problem in your personal life:

➤ Be sensitive to the effect your problem will have on the work environment

➤ Be mindful of the work that must be accomplished

➤ Do not burden co-workers with every detail of your troubles

Some people take a personal challenge and turn it into a career advantage.

Connie, a corporate executive in her 50s, was being torn apart by her 30-year-old son who was constantly in trouble. Rather than drive her friends away by talking about it, she decided to devote most of her energy to her career. She said: "I cannot control the life of my son, but I can enhance my own through a good career."

If co-workers tell you about problems they are having in their personal lives, decide the level of support you are comfortable offering. Your involvement might include:

➤ Casually inquiring, "How are things going?"

➤ Offering to help with work responsibilities

➤ Providing support outside the workplace

When Tracy's husband was diagnosed with a terminal illness, her co-workers rallied to support her. Several co-workers volunteered to cover her responsibilities and others assisted by offering to run errands for her. Together, the entire department was able to maintain a normal work schedule during this difficult time. When Tracy finally returned to work, she did so gratefully, knowing that her job had been kept intact and realizing what wonderful co-workers she had.

In Tracy's case each person benefited from an increased sense of commitment to getting the work done and being part of a supportive environment.

Preventing Common Misunderstandings

Sometimes, without realizing it, we fall into situations that needlessly turn people against us. Have any of the following happened to you?

Failure to Give Others a Second Chance

It is true that we do not always get a second chance to make a good impression. But we may lose more than we suspect when we refuse to give people a second chance to build a relationship with us.

When Brenda first met Cynthia—both were new managers hired from the outside—Cynthia mishandled their first few moments together. Rather than give Cynthia a second chance, Brenda decided not to pursue a relationship with her. A year later, when Cynthia became Brenda's supervisor, Brenda realized she had needlessly damaged her career.

Expecting Management to Provide Motivation

When we hold management responsible for providing us with productivity incentives to keep us positive, we usually miss the boat and wonder why things didn't turn out well.

Within two months after starting work, Sal decided no one cared about his productivity and he turned negative. His productivity dropped to below where it was when he first started. This led to a counseling session with his supervisor. She stated that the company was providing the best possible working environment and Sal was responsible for his attitude and motivation. Sal took exception to her advice and resigned. When his next job—which took him six months to get—provided a working environment less attractive than the one he left, Sal began to understand that attitude and motivation are "do-it-yourself" projects in all environments.

Releasing Frustrations

Psychologists tell us it is healthy to blow off a little steam now and then. But when this occurs in front of co-workers, relationships can be damaged.

Amanda became so frustrated with her supervisor two weeks ago that she stormed out of the office and did not return until the next day. Although the two of them later patched things up, there was little Amanda could do to restore relationships with co-workers who had witnessed the incident. Amanda had to learn the hard way to release her frustrations in a harmless manner away from work.

Part 1 Summary

❑ Many employees, including managers, underestimate the importance of building strong human relations. They do not bother to learn good human-relations skills and in the process slow their career progress.

❑ Human-relations competencies, of which there are many, are perhaps more important to career success than are technical skills.

❑ A positive attitude plays a key role in the success of human relationships.

❑ Good communication is the lifeblood of all strong relationships.

❑ One way to avoid damaging a relationship is not to be overly sensitive to minor personality differences at the other end of the relationship line.

❑ Using the Mutual Reward Theory will help build, maintain, and repair important relationships.

❑ Most employees weaken relationships when they are often late to work or absent, because others must do assigned work for them.

❑ How team members relate to each other is directly correlated to the ensuing productivity.

❑ Maintaining good human relations during career-plateau periods is critical to an employee's ability to progress at work.

❑ Employees who are *human-relations* smart make an honest attempt to repair damaged relationships by initiating positive action as soon as possible. They do this even when the other party is primarily at fault.

Repairing Damaged Relationships

Nothing in life is to be feared. It is only to be understood."

–Marie Curie

Being Willing to Repair a Relationship

Like abandoned old cars, many relationships are left unrepaired on the side of the road. Even when healing a relationship is important to an individual's career, often no real effort to fix things occur. Many people choose to walk away from a promising situation rather than work to fix a damaged relationship. It is sometimes difficult to understand why.

One reason may be that one party is reluctant or unwilling to discuss the matter. The only way to correct this is to initiate a conversation with that person. A comfortable way to do this is to make an open statement such as: "Our relationship is important to me, and I am anxious to know what it will take to repair and maintain it." Of course, every person must design an approach that is comfortable. To assist you in initiating such a discussion, try one of the following tips:

➤ Find something amusing to share

➤ Become a better listener

➤ Be willing to give a little more than you receive

➤ Let the other party save face

The healing of any relationship rests on both parties' willingness to try. With honest willingness on your part, you may discover the same attitude on the other side. Simply making the effort to talk about fixing things could turn you into a human-relations winner.

Is there a relationship in your career that could benefit from healing? If yes, set a date to take the first step.

What do you really have to lose?

EVALUATE YOUR EAGERNESS TO RESTORE THE RELATIONSHIP

Most relationship conflicts are repairable. A few are not. Often individuals are so ambivalent about trying to restore a relationship that they back away without making an effort. The purpose of the following exercise is to prevent you from doing this. If you come up with *yes* answers to many of the questions below, you should do your best to repair any damage no matter who caused it in the first place. Results will be best if you think about a *real* relationship conflict you are facing. Please answer all questions.

Your relationship conflict—ask yourself:	YES	NO
1. Is the relationship in question important to your future?	❏	❏
2. Has the relationship been rewarding in the past?	❏	❏
3. Are you willing to communicate openly about the conflict?	❏	❏
4. Are you willing to discuss possible solutions with the other party?	❏	❏
5. Would you consider initiating a meeting with the other person regardless of how the conflict started?	❏	❏
6. If your attempt to repair the relationship fails, will you feel defeated?	❏	❏
7. If the repairing effort fails, will others be disappointed?	❏	❏
8. Do you honestly want the party at the other end of the relationship line to feel that the relationship has been resolved?	❏	❏
9. Can you ignore irritating personality traits to repair the relationship?	❏	❏
10. Can you forgive and forget?	❏	❏

Number of *yes* answers _____

Scoring:

If you gave eight or more *yes* answers, the possibility of repairing the relationship is excellent. You should not hesitate to arrange a meeting. Four or more *yes* answers indicate the possibility is very good. Giving three or fewer *yes* answers is a signal that repairing the relationship may be a long shot.

Opening Up the Relationship for Discussion

If good communication is the lifeblood of any healthy relationship, then a transfusion of free, open communication should be the first order of business in any relationship repair. It is important to select the right time—when you think the other party will be receptive—and the right place, private and free from interruptions and maybe a neutral location. In addition, the discussion should open in a quiet, nonthreatening manner.

Once the time and place are right and both parties are comfortable, you should state in your own way that you would like to discuss a "win-win" that will repair the relationship and keep it healthy. You should invite the other party to describe what it will take to adjust the system so that both of you will benefit.

It took Jessica three days to gather up her nerve and select the right time to open a discussion with Hayden over their recent falling out. Although she felt nervous in getting the conversation going, they were able to discuss the events that had led to their misunderstanding. They both soon realized they had failed to keep each other in the loop on the new product development timeline. Through the discussion, they came up with a better plan to keep each other informed on the project's progress in a way that would improve their working relationship.

The Mutual Reward Theory, or "win-win," is only one approach that can be used to repair a relationship. You may want to employ another that fits better into your comfort zone.

Resolving Conflicts

In his book *Team Building: An Exercise in Leadership*, Robert B. Maddux points out many styles in conflict resolution as illustrated in the following matrix.

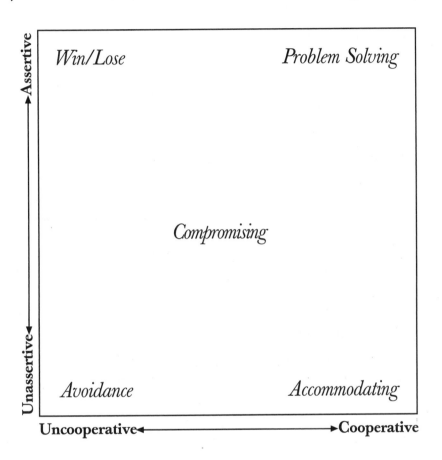

According to this graphic, if you are:

➤ Unassertive and uncooperative, your conflict resolution style is *avoidance*

➤ Unassertive and cooperative, you are *accommodating*

➤ Assertive and uncooperative, you play a *win/lose* game

➤ Assertive and cooperative, you are likely to solve your problems

Even when differences exist, the key is willingness to *compromise*.

Compromising to Ward Off Conflict

In most one-on-one situations, some compromise is necessary to maintain the relationship. Sometimes a little give from one end will do the trick. More often both parties must soften their position from time to time.

Why is compromise often so difficult?

One reason may be that many people establish such rigid and defiant positions to begin with that they would interpret any compromise as weakness or failure.

Greg took such a firm stand with his manager about not accepting a temporary assignment that he could not make himself compromise. Later he discovered his stand had caused a serious conflict and he had second thoughts about compromising, but it was too late.

From an MRT perspective, a *compromise* often simply means shifting some benefits or rewards. Rather than giving in and perhaps losing face, one party may agree to provide a different reward than anticipated in exchange for a substitute that is better than the one currently being received.

Under a corporate flextime schedule, Gillian wanted to delay arriving at work until 9 A.M. so she could drop her daughter off at school. The only one in the department Gillian could find to cover for her was Sandy, who was single. When Gillian asked her for the favor, Sandy was testy about making the change until the manager explained that the earlier starting time would give Sandy an opportunity to operate a new machine that would improve her skills. Sandy quickly compromised and accepted the new work schedule.

When there is a standoff between two people, a substitution of rewards sometimes can create two winners.

Rebuilding a Relationship with Your Supervisor

Your most important working relationship is with your immediate supervisor. If something damages this sensitive relationship—no matter who is at fault—immediate repair work is necessary.

How do you go about this?

The first thing to remember is that you do not want to allow a small injury to become a major one. Think through the issue. Just how are you affected? Test your perceptions with a friend who is qualified to weigh the problem from a more objective point of view.

Second, select the right time to approach your supervisor. On any given day, other priorities or problems may interfere with time to talk with you. If so, wait it out. Pick a time and place when you can talk freely and your supervisor has time to talk things out.

Remember that not all supervisors are comfortable with their roles. In fact, most people are not well-trained in conflict resolution. They may genuinely want to be sensitive and fair, but lack of experience, technique, or pressures interfere. Do not expect perfection. Be satisfied with the best repair job that is possible under the circumstances.

Keep in mind that you should be more interested in repairing the relationship than in getting your supervisors to change their behavior to accommodate your needs. All your co-workers are entitled to their personalities, just as you are entitled to yours.

When rebuilding a relationship with a supervisor, use the following suggestions to help you reach a full restoration:

➤ Keep your personal productivity high

➤ Maintain positive relationships with your co-workers

➤ Communicate through your attitude that you value your work

➤ Refuse to bad-mouth your supervisor in front of others

If you permit a supervisor to intimidate you, a healthy two-way relationship will be impossible. But intimidation by a supervisor is not likely, because most know they are measured by their staff's performance.

CASE STUDY: RELATIONSHIP REPAIR LEADS TO REWARD

Three years ago Jim was promoted to office manager in a large financial institution. He quickly discovered his new supervisor Shelly had trouble communicating. Shelly was abrupt and did not seem at all interested in Jim's career.

When Jim told his wife about Shelly's communication problems, she suggested he schedule a time with her to discuss how they could best work together. At the first opportunity, Jim asked Shelly what he could contribute in his new role. The next day, Jim summarized Shelly's expectations and delivered a list of work-oriented goals based on her comments. Jim asked for her critique.

As he began delivering some of the output Shelly wanted, the elements he wanted, such as more open communication, slowly began to come through. Eventually, a solid relationship emerged. Jim was recently named as Shelly's replacement when she was promoted.

In using the MRT approach, did Jim avoid a conflict?

Compare your answer to the authors' suggested
response in the back of the book.

Dealing with Sharks

Near every school of salt-water fish, you find a few sharks or other predators. Likewise, in every work environment you are apt to find a similar overly aggressive (sometimes unscrupulous) co-worker. These individuals can be so devious and insensitive that it does not bother them to make you, or others, victims.

How do you deal with these "sharks"?

First, understand that predators usually thrive on passive souls. At first, they may appear hostile to those who stand up to them—harsh reactions are typical—but often they silently respect, or even fear, competitors. So the first thing to do is let sharks know they will have trouble making a victim out of you. When forced, you, too, can be tough.

Vanessa was using every technique in the book to undercut Patsy to get the new job that co-workers knew Patsy had earned. She talked about Patsy to others in a very condescending tone. She gossiped about Patsy in ways that put Patsy in a bad light. She even tried to take credit for work Patsy had done. Then Patsy invited Vanessa for coffee and said: "Vanessa, my career is as important to me as yours is to you. I don't mind competition, but I want you to know that I do not intend to become a victim. Don't let the name Patsy fool you. I'm not. Fair?"

In building relationships with sharks, it is always a good idea to keep the following in mind:

➤ Do not expect your supervisor or co-workers to protect you

➤ After a confrontation, you can often build an improved relationship

➤ Those who have an emotional reaction after standing up to others should seek the support of people away from work to help diminish the side effects

 No one can make you feel inferior without your consent."

—Eleanor Roosevelt

CASE STUDY: BEING SWALLOWED BY A SHARK

Rob and Jordan started their careers in a large organization at the same time. It soon became obvious, however, that their philosophies toward work and career advancement were radically different.

A quiet, introspective person, Rob does his best to maintain soft, comfortable relationships in all directions. He wants to advance in the organization, but is not as eager as Jordan. Jordan is more competitive. She enjoys confrontations with Rob and others. Jordan has learned that if she can upset another person emotionally, she often comes out ahead. She has the ability to handle heated situations better than others do. Jordan does not feel guilty for using this technique. So far Jordan's strategy seems to be working. Although younger than Rob, she occupies a more responsible position.

How would you advise people like Rob to deal with those like Jordan?

_____

_____

_____

_____

_____

_____

_____

Compare your answers to the authors' suggested responses in the back of the book.

Part 2 Summary

❑ The first step in repairing a relationship is being willing to communicate.

❑ The Mutual Reward Theory approach to resolving a conflict may be your best bet.

❑ Conflict resolution usually includes some degree of compromise from each party.

❑ It often takes all of the tools in your repair kit to restore a relationship with a supervisor.

❑ "Sharks" are less likely to attack co-workers who stand up to them.

40

Protecting Yourself from Self-Sabotage

Skepticism is a hedge against vulnerability."

–Charles Thomas Samuels

42

Understanding Self-Sabotage

The premise of this book is that those who develop and practice sound human-relations competencies will enjoy greater career success. A corollary is that those who build healthy working relationships are less apt to *sabotage,* or hurt, themselves and those relationships.

This does not mean, however, that those who become human-relations smart and learn how to repair relationships effectively will not occasionally sabotage themselves in a conflict. They will! That is why this section is a significant aspect of human-relations education. Only by knowing how and why people unnecessarily sabotage themselves—and learning how to prevent it from happening to you—can you achieve the full benefits of *Winning at Human Relations.*

The Stages of Self-Sabotage

In most human-relations conflicts, you either work to repair relationships or you avoid the conflict and sabotage yourself. Once conflict avoidance begins, often both parties become increasingly involved in an emotional/psychological process that accelerates into higher and more damaging stages. The self-sabotage process has three stages:

Stage 1:   Surface damage with low hurt involvement within individuals. The prospects for healing are excellent if either party takes immediate action.

Stage 2:   Deeper damage to the relationship. Emotional hurt may be more serious within one individual than the other. Healing becomes more difficult. One or both parties may feel deep hurt.

Stage 3:   Emotional/psychological conflict is severe. Both parties are often hurt. Healing often depends on the willingness of both parties to communicate openly. Professional counseling may be needed.

The process varies depending on the individuals and the nature of the conflict. Once started, however, it often escalates until one or both parties lose. Even if one party wins, both feel the pain and the scars may be deep.

The sooner any damage, no matter how slight, is repaired, the better. Just as both individuals can lose, both can also win if they take proper timely action.

Acknowledging the Impact on Self and Career

When people are unfortunate enough to be victims of either an unintentional accident or a deliberate crime, they often pay a terrible price. The consequences can be similarly serious for victims of human-relations conflicts. In extreme cases, they can negatively affect lifelong career progress. Consider the following:

➤ Statistically, only a small percentage of people become victims of a serious crime. Everyone eventually becomes a victim of a damaged relationship.

➤ Financial loss from robbery, fraud, or physical injury can be high. So can the loss of a career opportunity.

➤ The emotional and psychological damage of being a human-relations victim can sometimes be as traumatic as being a crime victim.

Human conflicts can tear people apart emotionally. Often they are affected so much that their productivity drops. It is not unusual for people to turn negative and lose sight of their goals.

Last week Haley and Gina got into an argument over a minor matter involving work schedules. Emotions ran high. Gina adjusted within the hour, but Haley took the incident personally and sulked around the office for the rest of the week. Her productivity dropped and her supervisor noticed an uncustomary negative attitude toward co-workers and customers alike. In a human-relations sense, Gina outsmarted Haley by refusing to sabotage herself over a trivial matter.

All of us, on occasion, deal with fragile, awkward, human-relations situations. When we can handle these without sabotaging ourselves, we benefit. By learning how to deal with diverse personalities, we demonstrate we are human-relations smart and we become true winners.

Once a conflict occurs, your goal should be to repair the relationship as soon as possible without hurting yourself or the other party. It is difficult to make career progress if you leave a trail of damaged relationships behind you. And a primary concern should be the psychological damage you are capable of doing to yourself.

Human-relations mistakes—from which no one is immune—are damaging enough when we quickly resolve the issues. But when we internalize the conflict and sabotage ourselves, the damage is compounded. Thinking of yourself as a victim in a relationship can lead to moodiness, a loss of confidence, resentment, indignation, mental distress, and in extreme cases, violence.

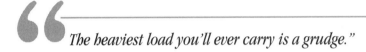

The heaviest load you'll ever carry is a grudge."

—Julie Alexander

HOW DO THESE SITUATIONS AFFECT YOU?

This exercise is designed to help you become more aware of how every-day situations can lead to self-sabotage. First, study each situation. Place a check (✔) by the situations you can relate to. Please add your own touchy points at the bottom. Do you have only a few check marks or are there many? Becoming aware of how various situations affect you will help you to eliminate self-sabotaging behavior.

- ✔ Embarrassing yourself by becoming publicly upset over slow service

- ❑ Replaying a minor human-relations mistake in your mind until you lose sleep over it

- ❑ Refusing to apologize over a small human-relations error

- ❑ Holding a grudge over a simple mistake made by another person

- ❑ Refusing to let another person apologize for being insensitive to you

- ✔ Becoming furious over a bill that seems too large or was sent in error

- ❑ Over-committing to one co-worker at the expense of damaging good relationships with other team members

- ✔ Getting frustrated with a computer or other device because it will not work properly for you

- ❑ Becoming frustrated trying to fight the bureaucracy at "city hall"

- ❑ Allowing someone who does not follow through to your expectations to increase your blood pressure

Other situations:

_____

_____

_____

Guarding Against Escalating Conflict

Self-sabotage can occur in many ways. Sometimes it comes from being overly sensitive to small matters, such as minor rebuffs, unintentional slights, and the like. At other times, major problems, such as deep-seated personality conflicts or prejudice, can cause severe damage to self-esteem. Self-sabotage also can occur when we permit conflicts away from work to spill over into the workplace and damage our careers. The following examples illustrate these three common ways people sabotage themselves.

Refusing to Correct Mistakes Quickly

Jose knew he had offended Randall when he neglected to include him in a decision-making meeting. Jose apologized quickly, stating how he valued their relationship, and invited Randall to lunch. Before lunch ended, the relationship had been fully restored.

Permitting a No-Fault Situation to Go Unanswered

It became obvious to everyone but Pascal that the misunderstanding was nobody's fault and a classic, almost laughable case of miscommunication. Even so, Rory, the only one who could be deeply hurt by the situation, played it safe and took Pascal out to lunch to discuss what happened and make certain their relationship was back on sound footing. When asked by a co-worker why he took the initiative, Rory replied: "Nobody was at fault, but I didn't want to gamble and wind up damaging our relationship because Pascal didn't see the big picture."

Permitting the Emotionalism of a Relationship Conflict to Chew You Up Inside

When Lionel and Andrew got into a conflict, Lionel internalized the situation to the point that he could not sleep at night. Soon his productivity dropped. Andrew, with more experience and objectivity, was able to pass off the emotional side more easily. Result? Lionel remained so bothered by the incident that he resigned, even though he liked his job. Lionel sabotaged himself.

More employees resign because of a relationship conflict than for any other reason. Has this ever happened to you?

ARE YOU SABOTAGING YOURSELF?

The temptation to blame others for normal human problems is natural. Listed below are typical workplace problems. As you read them, reflect on your behavior in the work environment. Do any of these scenarios apply to your behavior in the workplace?

➤ You blow off steam about an irritating habit of your supervisor and the word gets back to her.

➤ A co-worker is a know-it-all and you permit it to get under your skin.

➤ You and your manager have a fundamental communications misunderstanding over deadlines.

➤ A careless co-worker forgets to tell you about an important telephone call from a customer and you lose the account.

➤ Your manager, under pressure, comes down on you heavily in front of the office staff, but apologizes in private the next day.

➤ To your bitter disappointment, your request to attend an out-of-state meeting is turned down.

➤ You discover that your manager accepted an idea you discussed with a co-worker a few weeks ago and gave that person credit.

➤ You discover that a fellow employee has blown the whistle on you for unintentionally violating a safety rule.

If you tend to blame others in these situations, you could be sabotaging yourself. It is a difficult lesson to learn, but in building relationships it often does not matter who is at fault. When faced with similar situations in the future, why not ask yourself: Am I becoming a victim?

Choose one of the preceding scenarios that relates to your behavior at work. Take a moment to reflect and write what you could have done differently so this would not happen again.

_____

_____

Assessing Risk Level in a Relationship

Generally speaking, the more meaningful a relationship is, the more risk is involved for becoming deeply hurt when damage occurs. This is the *High Involvement High Vulnerability Principle*. It states that the more involved and intense a relationship becomes, the more vulnerable you are to being hurt if a conflict arises. The following three critical factors are involved in all working relationships:

Frequency of Contact

If you have a conflict with a person you work with daily, you are more apt to be hurt than if the conflict is with a more distant co-worker. Daily contact can intensify a conflict even though the opportunity for communication—and resolve—is present.

Nature of Relationship

Your relationship with your supervisor is far more complex than what you have with most co-workers. Such factors as authority, performance appraisals, and discipline are involved. Maintaining a relationship with a supervisor often requires more attention, care, and perception.

Personal Involvement

The better you know a co-worker personally, the more sensitive the situation can become if a conflict surfaces. This is the reason many experienced workers choose to keep their personal and working relationships separate.

Some working relationships require more maintenance than others do. Generally, high-involvement individuals are the people who will come to your support when needed. But they can also damage you the most in conflict situations.

Have you ever experienced the High Involvement High Vulnerability Principle?

> Your co-workers may express sympathy toward a relationship conflict you are experiencing while at the same time sitting back and wondering why you are so intent on sabotaging yourself.

Agreeing on Contributions to the Relationship

Outside of marriage, no arrangement places more demands on the Mutual Reward Theory than a 50/50 business partnership. This is true because the legal structure of a partnership is designed to establish an equal reward system that is nearly impossible to maintain. Each partner is supposed to contribute equal energy, talent, hours, and capital to the success of the business. When one partner perceives that the other is not contributing equally, a conflict can surface.

Beth and Carol Ann decided to open a day-care center as a 50/50 partnership. They spent hundreds of hours researching and planning the operation. But neither took time for a close look at the kind of relationship they could develop and maintain. Were they compatible? Did they understand the division of duties? Could they make it work? After both families contributed their savings—and took out second mortgages—they launched the operation with great success. The profit the first year was greater than either Beth or Carol Ann had hoped to achieve. Even so, the business eventually failed. Neither Beth nor Carol Ann could maintain an ongoing acceptable working relationship because neither could agree on the level of contribution the other was making to the business.

Few relationships demand as much as a business partnership, but *all* relationships have a stress factor. When the stress falls more heavily on one person than the other, that individual is vulnerable. Although Beth and Carol Ann experienced financial challenges because their business failed, the more serious damage was emotional because it broke up a 20-year friendship.

> " *Old roles are meant to be broken—especially when friendships turn into business partnerships.*"

—**Robin Thompson**

CASE STUDY: DISAGREEMENT LEADS TO SELF-SABOTAGE

Dr. Franklin was highly regarded by his colleagues at Apex University. He was treated with sensitivity and given every consideration. When he decided to expand his department, Professor Franklin was given immediate authority to recruit and hire an assistant.

After several interviews, he selected a much younger but highly qualified individual. For the first year, they appeared to have a solid working relationship. Then philosophical differences surfaced and students began to take sides with either Dr. Franklin or his assistant. Soon, the colleagues started to avoid each other. Then they stopped communicating completely. Without communication, the conflict intensified. Four years later, Dr. Franklin took early retirement to avoid further emotional stress. To those aware of what was going on, it became obvious that Dr. Franklin had retired to avoid the conflict.

What might Dr. Franklin have done in the early stages to avoid the conflict?

_____

_____

_____

What corrective steps might he have taken to restore the relationship?

_____

_____

_____

Is it fair to say that Dr. Franklin sabotaged himself?

_____

_____

_____

Compare your answers to the authors' suggested responses in the back of the book.

Knowing Your Vulnerability to Self-Sabotage

Sometimes it is important to defend a principle even though it is controversial and will create a conflict. Before taking such a position, however, you must consider whether you will sabotage yourself.

For many reasons (sibling rivalry, family training, cultural background, etc.) some people more easily let go of the emotions that accompany conflict. Others internalize the emotions and allow the conflict to seriously disrupt their lives.

Marci and Jasmine would go into a management meeting with the same amount of enthusiasm. If the meeting was without controversy, they would leave the same way they entered. If emotions ran high, however, Marci could let it go before leaving work, while Jasmine would lose sleep and not overcome the conflict's effect for several days.

Those who are unable to keep relationship conflicts from getting "under their skin" are more vulnerable to self-sabotage than those able to step back. Such individuals must learn to play their cards differently. This may mean taking a closer look at the principle to see if it is worth defending, preparing to remain more objective, or finding an acceptable compromise or substitute.

If you want to become a martyr to a principle, make sure the issue warrants it. Only when your values are being severely violated should you leave a job. If there is a difference of opinion, you must remember that you could be wrong. Study the opposing view with an open mind to make certain of your position. If you find you are wrong, turn this finding into a positive learning experience rather than a major career change.

Becoming a martyr in most business environments is a good way to botch your career progress permanently.

It is fine to stand on a principle that is important to you...providing you do not get so emotionally entangled that you sabotage yourself.

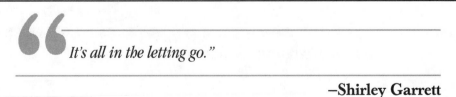

It's all in the letting go."

—**Shirley Garrett**

Looking at the Big Picture

When people discover they are in a relationship conflict, few have the insight or experience to back away from it and look at the bigger picture before trying to repair the damage. Learning how to do this might enable you to approach the same situation differently, with far better results.

Joe became so distressed over the relationship with his new supervisor that he almost resigned on the spot. Controlling his emotions, he and a friend took time to evaluate the conflict. When Joe and his friend assessed the situation from all angles (Joe's seniority, experience, corporate friends, image, etc.), it became clear that Joe would be adopting self-sabotaging behavior if he let his supervisor get to him. It was hard on Joe's ego but he decided to compromise and work to rebuild the relationship. Today Joe is a senior manager in the organization and his former supervisor is no longer with the company.

Warning Signs of Self-Sabotage

In the area of human relationships, it is often difficult to see the "forest"(your overall career) for all the "trees"(your current stresses). The following are three factors that can keep you from seeing the big picture.

Falling for the "Eye-for-an-Eye" Syndrome

When we are under stress from a relationship conflict, it is natural to blame the other person.

When the sales manager gave a choice sales territory to Bernadette, Frasier exploded. He laid the blame at the door of the sales manager. His hostility cost him being considered for assistant sales manager—a better opportunity than staying in the field—which was to be reviewed in a few weeks. As a result of the turmoil, Frasier resigned to save face. Looking back, Frasier knows he sabotaged himself and blew a good career possibility with a quality company.

Accepting Advice from the Wrong Sources

When a relationship conflict surfaces, it is possible to gain a better perspective by talking things over with another person, but not always. The wrong person can pour fuel on the fire and the situation can intensify, pushing both parties further from a solution.

Mia was so upset when Jeremy got the promotion that she needed to talk to someone. She chose Lindsay and Alison. Neither of them knew all the facts, and they persuaded Mia to file a sex-discrimination suit. The preliminary investigation showed Jeremy was more qualified and management had made a sound decision. By the time Mia backed away from the investigation, her relationship with Lindsay and Alison had ended. Mia realized she had unnecessarily sabotaged herself because of poor advice from two co-workers.

Talking out the issue with an *objective* observer (Lindsay and Alison were not objective) can dissipate some of the pain and better classify the issue. A few possibilities might be:

> ➤ Someone in the human-resources department

> ➤ A mentor

> ➤ A more senior person with whom you can share a confidence

> ➤ An outside source with similar work experience

Letting Your Ego Stand in the Way

Everyone makes mistakes in relationships. Sometimes even those with experience and positive self-esteem make simple misjudgments that might be expected of an inexperienced employee. When this happens, the "pro" ego can get in the way of finding a good solution.

Jacob found it humiliating when the quarterly report showed that Kayla, a new manager of a branch operation similar to his, had beaten his previous quarterly sales record. The next time he and Kayla met, Jacob was demeaning in his comments and initiated a conflict that became common knowledge around the firm. In the months that followed, Jacob tried so hard to beat Kayla that he neglected other aspects of his responsibilities. Eventually, the company president was forced to counsel Jacob. Result? Kayla got a promotion that could have been Jacob's had his ego not gotten in the way.

In the relationship conflict, it is very possible to "win a battle and lose the war." People can become so involved in the psychology of the conflict that they fail to recognize they are sabotaging themselves. That is why protecting yourself from the career damage that self-sabotage can inflict requires stepping back from current stresses and taking a look at the long-term picture.

"*Don't let your short-term problems interfere with your long-term goals.***"**

–Ken Alexander

CASE STUDY: QUALITY RELATIONSHIPS VS. QUANTITY

In all of her 32 years, Danielle had never felt more frustrated. Her career path had been placed on hold because of corporate downsizing, a trusted co-worker had done a number on her, and she was extremely upset by the conflict in her divorce proceedings that had been going on for several weeks.

Talking to her sister, Amber, she commented: "Sis, I've decided never to enter a serious relationship again. That way, when it doesn't work out I can toss it. Meaningful relationships in all aspects of my life have a way of kicking me in the face."

Amber replied: "Danielle, we all need meaningful relationships, both at work and in our personal lives. It's quality, not quantity. I believe you should stay in the mainstream and enjoy people. But you also must learn to grow up and find a way to develop and maintain good relationships. It's not the number of flowers in your garden; it's the beauty of those you nurture."

Amber told Danielle that her problem was that every time a relationship went bad, she felt sorry for herself and became more of a loner. Amber advised her that if she did not learn to build and protect rewarding relationships, she would continue to sabotage herself. "You are going to turn into a loner," Amber warned.

How is Danielle sabotaging herself?

_____

_____

_____

If Danielle were your friend or sister, what advice would you give her?

_____

_____

_____

Compare your answers to the authors' suggested responses in the back of the book.

Part 3 Summary

❑ The self-sabotaging process tends to accelerate unless immediate steps are taken to resolve the conflict.

❑ You sabotage yourself in a conflict—even if you are not at fault—when you think of yourself as helpless and ineffective.

❑ Self-sabotage occurs when you cannot handle the emotional strain that goes with a relationship conflict.

❑ Most people are so involved in the emotionalism of a conflict that they are unaware they are sabotaging themselves.

58

Putting It All Together into a Winning Strategy

" *Our major obligation is not to mistake slogans for solutions.* "

–Edward R. Murrow

60

Ten Techniques for Winning at Human Relations

Let's review what we have covered so far in this book. Part 1 explained that by following certain principles, you can build and maintain better relationships with supervisors and co-workers. Part 2 gave you a tested approach to use in repairing damaged relationships. Part 3 outlined how to protect yourself from self-sabotage in relationship conflicts.

Now that you understand these human-relations skills, you are ready to put what you have learned into a master strategy. This part presents 10 practical techniques that will help you effectively build and maintain quality relationships. By making progress in all directions, you can enhance your career progress and earn the compliment of being called *human-relations smart*.

You will be asked to reflect on each of the 10 techniques from your experience, insight, and personal style. Read the *reality-check* question at the end of each technique and circle either *yes* or *no* to reflect your response. Your answer may provide you with added insight about how you view relationships. Also provided is an optional self-awareness exercise that can provide you with a greater sense of self-understanding.

Technique 1: Create and Maintain a Variety of Relationships

In any job, there are many relationships to create and maintain. Besides supervisors and co-workers, usually clients and key people in other departments are also important to your career progress. An administrative assistant, security guard, or maintenance person should not be ignored.

Co-workers, however, deserve special attention for the following reasons:

➤ When you help fellow workers produce more, you enhance your reputation.

Although Tim's personal productivity was average, management recognized that he was always helping team members with technical problems, which contributed to their higher productivity.

➤ When you keep a good attendance record and show up on time each day, you make things easier for your supervisor and co-workers.

Although Anna was slower than others in serving customers, she was never late and seldom absent. Whenever another department member did not show, Anna picked up the slack without complaining.

➤ When co-workers like you, they can influence management to promote you.

Through her positive attitude, Sydney earned the respect of co-workers as well as supervisors. When the manager position opened up, three co-workers told management they could work well with Sydney.

Other relationships should not be neglected. But for those who want to impress management that they are human-relations smart, an excellent place to demonstrate such skills is with co-workers.

Reality Check

Do you strive to maintain a variety of relationships within the work environment? Check (✔) *yes* or *no*.

❑ Yes   ❑ No

Self-awareness exercise:

Keep a log of the relationships you are actively working to maintain. How much variety in departments do they represent? In levels of responsibility within the company? In diverse backgrounds and interests?

Technique 2: See Relationships, Not Personalities

You will take a major step in improving relationships and avoiding conflicts when you learn to concentrate on the relationship, not the personality at the end of the relationship line. Easy to say, sometimes hard to accomplish!

Marla had high personal standards of grooming and social grace. She could find little right with her co-worker Kent. Without sensing the negative implications, she often tore him down in public by commenting on his lack of polish. When her supervisor suggested she look at the contribution Kent was making to the department and not at his personal habits of dress or imperfect grammar, her attitude started to change. Although Marla would not choose to mix socially with Kent, she recognized that he was a career professional with many unique talents.

To keep working relationships in good order, it is best to observe what people do rather than what they seem to be on the surface. Work habits, not minor personality quirks, are important on the job. Do your colleagues do their best to carry a full load? Do they cooperate and work well with others? Are they willing to learn? Do they have special talents that contribute to team productivity?

Professional employees should deal with working relationships and attempt to stay away from a critical analysis of personalities. Those who deal in what can be called "personality assassinations" create human conflicts and can easily wind up sabotaging themselves.

Reality Check

Can you separate a colleague's personality from his or her work contributions? Check (✔) *yes* or *no*.

❑ Yes   ❑ No

Self-awareness exercise:
Pay attention to the times you stereotype people. Then select one of these individuals that you see regularly and assume for the next several encounters, that the *opposite* of your stereotypic belief is true. How did this make you feel about the person?

Technique 3: Practice the Mutual Reward Theory

For a one-on-one session with an individual with whom you share a conflict, a direct approach is not always the best. For many people a confrontation may be too stressful and uncomfortable. Answer? Initiate a discussion that develops a *mutual reward* approach.

As you learned earlier, the Mutual Reward Theory states that for a human relationship to remain healthy over an extended time, the benefits must be balanced between both parties. What is important is that both participants view what they receive from the relationship as satisfactory to them. Both should feel they come out ahead. The idea is to introduce the mutual reward concept with the other party.

> *Jackson, sensing that his on-the-job relationship with Shawna was deteriorating, set up a meeting in her office and said: "Shawna, until now we have worked well together. But I get the feeling we are beginning to work against each other instead of pulling together. I would like to get your ideas on how we can keep our mutual support system working."*

Using the mutual reward concept takes an oblique rather than confrontational approach. Not only is it easier to use, but with open communication, a more satisfactory reward mix usually develops. In almost all relationship conflicts, reconciliation depends on the creation of a more satisfactory reward system. This is the true meaning of give and take or compromise in conflict resolution.

Reality Check

Do you work to resolve conflicts so both people will benefit? Check (✔) *yes* or *no*.

❏ Yes ❏ No

Self-awareness exercise:
Think of a recent situation in which mutual rewards were in jeopardy. What did you do to resolve the situation so both people benefited?

Technique 4: Let Small Irritations Pass

Adam and his wife were waiting for a valet to bring their car to the front of a restaurant where they had enjoyed a delightful dinner. When the car arrived, Adam noticed a large dent in the rear fender and immediately blew his top. After embarrassing both his wife and himself, he discovered the valet had brought another customer's car that was identical to theirs. Their car was fine. Adam did not sleep well that night, but it was his own fault. He had blown his stack before properly assessing the situation. He had sabotaged himself.

How many times have you seen people come away the winner after making a fuss over slow service in a restaurant or complaining to a postal employee? Did they really win when they told somebody off on the telephone, became angry in a traffic jam, or worse, exploded in the work environment?

You might feel it is good to blow off some steam, but in most such cases, short-fuse individuals either hurt their image or wind up embarrassed and feeling foolish. And if you blow up over a minor irritation that was nobody's fault and then recognize it later as being dumb, it could ruin the rest of your day. The truth is, even though your complaint may have been justifiable, *you* look out of control, not the other party. How can you prevent this?

➤ Work on detaching yourself emotionally from upsetting trivial events. Tell yourself over and over that big people handle little irritations with grace.

➤ Train yourself to look beyond such incidents. One way to accomplish this is to walk away from the irritation, counting and reminding yourself that life is too short to worry about minor annoyances. You have more important things to do.

Reality Check

Do you let small irritations become big deals? Check (✔) *yes* or *no*.

❑ Yes   ❑ No

Self-awareness exercise:

Recall three situations in which you got upset. How would the person you most admire handle them? How did you handle them? What about each situation did you take personally?

Technique 5: Recognize Warning Signals

Many people fail to recognize the warning signs of a troubled relationship. Their feelings get hurt, and they blame the other party and react without considering the long-term effects. Some people follow this pattern over and over. How can you learn to warn yourself before excessive damage is done to an important relationship?

A first step is to ask the questions:

➤ Do I have more to lose than the other party?

➤ Is there still a chance to salvage the relationship?

➤ Is open communication still a possibility?

The best early warning signal is to stay aware of your attitude. Are you starting to react negatively to a person or situation? Are you as positive about your career and the work environment as you were previously?

On his last appraisal, Roger was given a satisfactory rating on attitude. His previous rating had been superior. When Roger asked why, he was told that his enthusiasm and sensitivity to others seemed to have diminished measurably. Thinking back to a relationship problem that had surfaced in his department, Roger recognized that this was when he had started to turn negative, and the change in rating was justified.

Every individual is the custodian of his or her attitude. You cannot expect others to tell you when it turns from positive to negative. But if you are honest and in touch with yourself, you know when it happens. When you sense things are out of tune, evaluate why you feel that way. Your negative attitude may be the best signal that you have to begin rebuilding a relationship before it is too late.

Reality Check

Do you strive to recognize and then repair relationships? Check (✔) *yes* or *no*.

❑ Yes ❑ No

Self-awareness exercise:
Try an experiment. For one day, smile and be positive and upbeat with everyone you encounter, even strangers. Pay attention to how they respond.

Technique 6: Choose Advisers Carefully

When relationship conflicts develop, you may feel a critical need to talk things over with others who can be objective. It is also therapeutic to do this. Whom should you select? On what basis?

Common sense tells us that it is smart to keep home-based problems away from work and some work problems away from home. This is especially true when you need to discuss a conflict involving a co-worker or family member. For example, it is probably best to discuss a serious work conflict with a mature outsider such as a spouse, friend, or professional counselor, unless you have an outstanding relationship with the co-worker(s) with whom you are in conflict. But talking freely about a home problem with co-workers may hurt productivity, your image, or possibly your relationships at home, especially if word gets back that you have been discussing details of your home life.

Either way, the problem comes in selecting the right person to assist you and provide objectivity. Those closest to you may be your logical first choice. But if they are not objective, taking their advice could do more harm than good.

When Maria had a home problem, her two best friends at work tried to offer advice based on their experiences. Maria welcomed their support, but it only intensified the situation at home and caused confusion and a loss of productivity at work. The delay damaged her ability to concentrate at work until she eventually found a solution through professional help.

So what is the answer? Discretion!

Choose your confidants carefully so your problem will not spill over and disturb other relationships at home or at work. The following suggestions may help.

➤ Select an adviser who understands self-sabotage and is far enough removed from the problem to be objective

➤ Try not to settle on any advice unless both parties in the conflict stand a chance of coming out ahead

➤ Be true to yourself and your judgment

➤ If you receive assistance from a friend, consider the help you received a reward and try to return it in the future

Reality Check

Do you have a trusted adviser or mentor that can guide you when you need to talk things over? Check (✔) *yes* or *no*.

❏ Yes   ❏ No

Self-awareness exercise:

Think of a time when you needed advice. Whom did you select? As you reflect on this situation, was that your best choice? Would you have selected another person if you were to do it over? What lesson can you gain from the experience that could be helpful the next time?

Technique 7: Distance Yourself from Unresolvable Conflict

When a relationship is important to your career, it is best to use good communication to repair any conflict. But what do you do when you sense conflict coming from those who are interested only in their gains and do not really care about you?

In recent weeks Jackie has been aware that her co-worker Aaron has been using her to further his career. He disrupts her productivity to ask about things he should be learning on his own time. He asks her to cover for him while he is playing office politics elsewhere. He is generous in buying drinks after work, but almost all of the conversation is directed to subjects that will enhance his career, not hers. Slowly, Jackie has decided that their relationship is never going to be mutually rewarding.

How can Jackie keep this imbalance from continuing or getting worse? Withdrawing from any relationship—rather than trying to resolve the conflict—can be a mixed blessing. When you feel you have had enough, follow these tips to distance yourself from the relationship:

➤ Go about it slowly even though the co-worker may suspect what is happening

➤ Be human-relations smart by becoming more involved with other co-workers to strengthen other relationships

➤ Consider changing lunch and after-work habits so you will have less contact with the difficult individual

Reality Check

Do you follow your instinct when you feel you should withdraw from a relationship? Check (✔) *yes* or *no*.

❑ Yes   ❑ No

Self-awareness exercise:

Select a relationship from which you have distanced yourself. Did it go smoothly? What different approach or technique might you have used to make the situation less stressful?

Technique 8: Know When to Compromise

If you react to any conflict by engaging in an "eye-for-an-eye" philosophy, you will quickly sabotage yourself by damaging other relationships. Your goal should be either to leave the individual alone or help that person win—even if he or she created the conflict—because it is the only way you can win.

When Jason heard that Thalia would receive the promotion he expected, his first reaction was to tell his co-workers she was a poor choice. Then, realizing that would look like sour grapes and potentially damage other relationships, Jason changed his mind. Two months later he received a promotion better suited to his talents. Both he and Thalia came out ahead.

Compromising to protect your future without hurting others is human-relations smart for many reasons, including the following:

➤ Conflicts that hurt others can boomerang if management senses productivity has lowered

➤ Others never respect vindictive behavior

➤ Compromising may generate new rewards that you value as much as or more than those you lose

➤ When you accept new ideas in a compromise, you benefit

➤ Compromise may be the only way to restore a relationship

Reality Check

Do you know when compromising is in your best interest? Check (✔) *yes* or *no*.

❏ Yes ❏ No

Self-awareness exercise:

Think of a situation where you chose to comprise. Did it help the situation? What would have happened if you had failed to compromise? How would your career have been affected?

Technique 9: Have a *Plan B* Ready

In today's world, career challenges can develop from two basic sources:

➤ A human relations problem left unsolved

➤ An organizational change

As insurance against either possibility, you should have an alternative career option known as a *Plan B**.

This book covers human-relations problems, not organizational changes. But organizational changes are more frequent today than ever before. Mergers, downsizing, restructuring, and technological advances have increased the intensity of change. Job security is no longer a given. Even if you play it human-relations smart, outside influences have the potential to cause problems that make a career change necessary or advisable.

What is a Plan B? It is simply a thoughtful strategy that can be activated on the day you decide on a career change. A professional Plan B is a formalized, comprehensive career-enhancement program that includes the following action steps:

➤ Ensure that you are as efficient as possible in your present job (Plan A)

➤ Keep your job competencies current so you always maintain your marketability

➤ Activate a creative networking system to help you locate other, potentially better opportunities

Because relationship conflicts are always present and organizational change will continue to intensify, experts today are advising that a career Plan B is a necessity, not an option.

---

*More information can be found in the Crisp Publications book, *Plan B: Converting Change into Career Opportunity*, by Elwood N. Chapman.

Reality Check

Do you have a Plan B? Check (✔) *yes* or *no*.

❏ Yes   ❏ No

Self-awareness exercise:
Review your Plan B as if it were not your plan, but a friend's. Take a critical look at job experience, professional development, and networking. Is the Plan B strong and ready to use at any time, or is it stagnant and out-of-date? What would you advise your friend to do to improve the plan?

Technique 10: Protect Your Attitude

Most employees are positive when on the job. Their positive, cooperative attitudes contribute to their productivity and that of their co-workers. Mature individuals recognize that the moment they turn negative, it signals the potential for trouble, including self-sabotage.

Attitude-conscious employees are aware of the negative career consequences that reside in a poor attitude. They know it is their personal responsibility to stay as upbeat and productive as possible, no matter what their home or work problems may be. The following techniques from *Attitude: Your Most Priceless Possession* will help you stay positive:

Use the Flipside Technique

When an irritating problem hits, "flip it over" to see if you can find some humor to soften the blow.

> *When Rick discovered someone had creased a fender in his car in the employee parking lot, he laughingly announced that he would buy the culprit a drink if his insurance protection would help him buy the new car he was already thinking about.*

This technique—even if you do not find any humor—may keep you from feeling like a victim.

Play Your Winners

Concentrate on the good things you have going for you so negative issues seem smaller.

> *Melinda, having a problem with her supervisor, stayed positive by writing down something good about her job every time she became upset with him. After exhausting all of the positive things she could think of (seven), she decided her job was better than she thought and initiated a meeting with her supervisor to see if things could be improved through better communication.*

Insulate Yourself Against Major Worries

When a major problem starts to pull you down, it is possible to push it to the outer perimeter of your mind so it will not interfere with your productivity.

Deanna, a popular and respected worker, had to take a week off when her only son was severely injured in an accident. Upon her return, she forced herself to think work instead of hospital and discovered it really helped her get through the difficult period.

Share Your Positive Attitude with Others

Little can dissipate a negative attitude faster than doing something special for another person.

Six months ago when Will turned negative over a family matter, he brought himself back by doing something special for a different person at work each day. Most of the time it was nothing more than a friendly compliment or an appropriate joke. Now Will maintains his positive attitude in the same way he recovered it.

Look Better to Yourself

One way to fight back when you are feeling down in the dumps is to improve your image.

When Kristen permitted her attitude to slip during a plateau period that she had not anticipated, she restored it by creating a new image through hairstyle, wardrobe, and a weight-loss program. When sales improved in her organization, she was immediately promoted.

When it comes to winning at human relations, attitude is your most priceless possession. Anything you can do to keep it consistently positive is a good investment.

This content was used with permission from *Attitude: Your Most Priceless Possession*, by Elwood N. Chapman and Wil McKnight, by Crisp Publications.

Reality Check

Is your attitude worth catching? Check (✔) *yes* or *no*.

❏ Yes   ❏ No

Self-awareness exercise:

Attitudes are contagious. Imagine you have been appointed the "attitude officer" for your company. What could you do today to improve your attitude and that of other employees? What could you do to improve the attitude for the next month or the year?

A P P E N D I X

" *A little learning is a dangerous thing, but a lot of ignorance is just as bad.* "

–Bob Edwards

Final Review Questions and Answers

1. **When it comes to human relations, I get the idea that an ounce of prevention is worth a pound of cure. Am I right?**

   Absolutely! Once self-sabotage starts, it is difficult to contain. Thus, the better you become at maintaining relationships, the fewer conflicts you will face.

2. **Wouldn't the passage of time cause some working relationship conflicts to disappear without action from either party?**

   Sometimes, but not always. And even when it does happen, a great deal of distress and loss of productivity could have occurred before time pushed the conflict into the distance. Open communication at the beginning can often keep this from happening.

3. **What kind of commitment is necessary to win at human relations?**

   A sincere, determined three-part commitment: (1) Continue to improve your human relations skills, (2) Use MRT to restore any broken relationships, and (3) Recognize that the moment you lose your positive attitude, you are sabotaging yourself.

4. **Is it possible for someone to remain sufficiently positive during a long-term relationship conflict at home so co-workers will not be negatively affected?**

   When off-the-job problems are severe, it usually affects job performance. That is one reason employee-assistance programs, supported by management, can contribute to productivity.

5. **If people are not accustomed to confronting others who are trying to sabotage them, won't taking such a step take an emotional toll?**

   Temporarily, yes, but the damage from permitting an intimidating relationship to continue could be far greater. Another advantage to confronting others is that it probably will not be so difficult, or damaging, the next time it is necessary.

6. **When is enough enough? When should a conflict cause an individual to pack up and leave a job or organization?**

   Once the sabotaging process between a supervisor and a worker reaches an advanced stage, it may be time to seek a transfer or look to another firm. A conflict between two co-workers may deserve a softer treatment. All of this assumes that attempts to heal the relationship have occurred.

RETEST YOUR HUMAN RELATIONS "SMARTS"

Demonstrate that you are human-relations smart by completing the following exercise. Write a *T* for each statement you consider true and an *F* for those you think are false. Correct answers are listed at the end of the exercise.

T **1.** The challenge is to make the most of human relationships without sabotaging yourself.

F **2.** Most people automatically know how to balance their technical and human relations skills.

F **3.** People can be more objective dealing directly with personalities rather than focusing on relationships.

T **4.** A mutually rewarding relationship is one in which both parties receive somewhat-equal but different benefits from each other.

T **5.** A conflict point in a relationship can occur when one party receives or gives too many rewards.

F **6.** MRT is a poor approach to use in the healing of a damaged relationship.

F **7.** Fortunately, the attitude of one employee does not influence the productivity of another.

T **8.** The key to restoring any damaged relationship is the willingness of both parties to try.

F **9.** Deciding whether to try to repair a damaged relationship depends on who was at fault.

T **10.** People who are human-relations smart never sabotage themselves.

F **11.** Embarrassing yourself in public does not come under the category of self-sabotage.

T **12.** Employees often set themselves up for more problems when they refuse to mend a repairable relationship quickly.

T **13.** The more meaningful a relationship, the less apt a person is to be sabotaged by it.

F **14.** Standing on principle does not involve human-relationship risks.

—CONTINUED—

CONTINUED

X

___T___ 15. Business partnerships create few conflicts.

___T___ 16. Self-sabotage usually occurs when a person cannot handle the emotional strain that goes with a relationship conflict.

___F___ 17. Absenteeism seldom leads to career damage.

___F___ 18. To resolve a severely damaged work-related relationship, it is always best to cut your losses by starting over elsewhere.

___T___ 19. A Plan B can help you be prepared for a major organizational change.

___T___ 20. Becoming negative may be an early warning that you are sabotaging yourself.

82

Authors' Suggested Responses to Case Studies

Case Study: Downplaying a Personality Conflict (page 7)

Jeff has too much invested with his firm not to give his wife's suggestion a serious try. If he resigns or takes early retirement, he could be sabotaging himself while the company president gets off free. Once Jeff stops talking about the president's irritating characteristics—and stops reinforcing them in his mind—he will be better able to concentrate on his responsibilities. This, in turn, will be therapeutic. The relationships between Jeff and the president may never be fully repaired, but by becoming more objective, Jeff should be able to survive without tearing himself up emotionally until normal personnel changes eliminate the problem. Jeff has already sabotaged himself, but his actions could cut his losses and restore the upward mobility of his career.

Case Study: Conflicting Relationships (page 19)

Although difficult, open communication with Victoria at the beginning could have enabled Jennifer to keep their working and social relationships separate. Professional employees are successful at doing this all the time. Lack of people experience was probably the reason it took Jennifer so long to catch on. In most work environments it is impossible for a high-productivity employee to carry a low-productivity employee without risk of damage to the high-productivity individual's image and career progress.

Case Study: Relationship Repair Leads to Reward (page 36)

Sometimes a positive approach to a potential relationship conflict is the only way to keep from sabotaging yourself. Jim may have saved his career by taking early action. His wife deserves credit for recommending the MRT approach.

Case Study: Being Swallowed by a Shark (page 38)

To protect their careers, non-assertive people like Rob need to train themselves to stand up to confrontation without sabotaging themselves. The fact that all-day seminars are often devoted to the process suggests it is not easy to learn. The following pattern might help Rob get started:

1. Discuss the situation with an objective adviser who is more experienced in confrontations.

2. With the help of this individual, design a strategy that minimizes the possibility of greater conflict.

3. Employ this strategy in a calm manner, without rancor or vindictiveness.

4. Whatever happens, do not take it personally.

5. Return to the original adviser to evaluate results so that improvements continue.

Case Study: Disagreement Leads to Self-Sabotage (page 51)

Early and open communication between Dr. Franklin and his assistant could have resolved their philosophical differences before a conflict spilled over onto students. Dr. Franklin should have taken the initiative. The MRT approach could have resolved the conflict. It is fair to say Dr. Franklin sabotaged himself. He should have reminded himself that communication is the lifeblood of any relationship and taken the first step.

Case Study: Quality Relationships vs. Quantity (page 56)

Danielle is sabotaging herself by engaging in negative self-talk that tells her not to enter into a serious relationship again. Her inner voice is replaying the tape of how she has been hurt, and it reminds her to avoid the pain by avoiding serious relationships. Amber has done an excellent job of pointing out the positive aspects of relationships. She has shared her insight on how to nurture relationships and has provided a glimpse into Danielle's future if she chooses to avoid meaningful relationships.

Recommended Reading

Bonet, Diana. *The Business of Listening, Third Edition.* Menlo Park, CA: Crisp Publications, 2001.

Chapman, Elwood, and Wil McKnight. *Attitude: Your Most Priceless Possession, Fourth Edition.* Menlo Park, CA: Crisp Publications, 2002.

Helmstetter, Shad, Ph.D. *What to Say When You Talk to Yourself.* NY: Pocket Books, 1982.

Kravitz, Michael, Ph.D., and Susan Schubert, M.A. *Emotional Intelligence Works.* Menlo Park, CA: Crisp Publications, 2000.

Lloyd, Sam. *Developing Positive Assertiveness, Third Edition.* Menlo Park, CA: Crisp Publications, 2002.

Lloyd, Sam, and Tina Berthelot. *Self-Empowerment, Revised Edition.* Menlo Park, CA: Crisp Publications, 2003.

Luhn, Rebecca, Ph.D. *Managing Anger.* Menlo Park, CA: Crisp Publications, 1992.

Maddux, Robert, and Barb Wingfield. *Team Building, Fourth Edition.* Menlo Park, CA: Crisp Publications, 2003.

Palladino, Connie, Ph.D. *Developing Self-Esteem.* Menlo Park, CA: Crisp Publications, 1994.

NOTES

NOTES

CRISP WORLDWIDE DISTRIBUTION

English language books are distributed worldwide. Major international distributors include:

ASIA/PACIFIC

Australia/New Zealand: In Learning, PO Box 1051, Springwood QLD, Brisbane, Australia 4127   Tel: 61-7-3-841-2286, Facsimile: 61-7-3-841-1580 ATTN: Messrs. Richard/Robert Gordon

Hong Kong/Mainland China: Crisp Learning Solutions, 18/F Honest Motors Building 9-11 Leighton Rd., Causeway Bay, Hong Kong   Tel: 852-2915-7119, Facsimile: 852-2865-2815 ATTN: Ms. Grace Lee

Indonesia: Pt Lutan Edukasi, Citra Graha, 7th Floor, Suite 701A, Jl. Jend. Gato Subroto Kav. 35-36, Jakarta 12950 Indonesia Tel: 62-21-527-9060/527-9061 Facsimile: 62-21-527-9062 ATTN: Mr. Suwardi Luis

Japan: Phoenix Associates, Believe Mita Bldg., 8th Floor 3-43-16 Shiba, Minato-ku, Tokyo 105-0014, Japan   Tel: 81-3-5427-6231, Facsimile: 81-3-5427-6232 ATTN: Mr. Peter Owans

Malaysia, Philippines, Singapore: Epsys Pte Ltd., 540 Sims Ave #04-01, Sims Avenue Centre, 387603, Singapore   Tel: 65-747-1964, Facsimile: 65-747-0162 ATTN: Mr. Jack Chin

CANADA

Crisp Learning Canada, 60 Briarwood Avenue, Mississauga, ON L5G 3N6 Canada Tel: 905-274-5678, Facsimile: 905-278-2801 ATTN: Mr. Steve Connolly

EUROPEAN UNION

England: Flex Learning Media, Ltd., 9-15 Hitchin Street, Baldock, Hertfordshire, SG7 6AL, England Tel: 44-1-46-289-6000, Facsimile: 44-1-46-289-2417   ATTN: Mr. David Willetts

INDIA

Multi-Media HRD, Pvt. Ltd., National House, Floor 1, 6 Tulloch Road, Appolo Bunder, Bombay, India 400-039 Tel: 91-22-204-2281, Facsimile: 91-22-283-6478 ATTN: Messrs. Ajay Aggarwal/ C.L. Aggarwal

SOUTH AMERICA

Mexico: Grupo Editorial Iberoamerica, Nebraska 199, Col. Napoles, 03810 Mexico, D.F. Tel: 525-523-0994, Facsimile: 525-543-1173   ATTN: Señor Nicholas Grepe

SOUTH AFRICA

Corporate: Learning Resources, PO Box 2806, Parklands, Johannesburg 2121, South Africa, Tel: 27-21-531-2923, Facsimile: 27-21-531-2944 ATTN: Mr. Ricky Robinson

MIDDLE EAST

Edutech Middle East, L.L.C., PO Box 52334, Dubai U.A.E. Tel: 971-4-359-1222, Facsimile: 971-4-359-6500   ATTN: Mr. A.S.F. Karim